Cast from Darkness

Published by
Mind's Eye Publications
985 Deborah Avenue
Elgin, IL 60123-1918

Cover Illustration by Marge Simon

ISBN 979-8-9887924-3-7
$8.00 US

Cast from Darkness

Poems by
Marge Simon
&
Mary Turzillo

Marge Simon lives in Ocala, Florida, with her husband, poet/writer Bruce Boston and the ghosts of two cats. She has won Multiple Bram Stoker Awards, Rhysling Awards, the Elgin, Dwarf Stars and Strange Horizons Readers' Award. She received HWA's Lifetime Achievement Award in 2021. Marge's poems and stories have appeared in *Asimov's, Magazine of F&SF, New Myths, Daily Science Fiction*. Her stories also appear in anthologies such as the 2020 Bookfest Award winning *Under Her Skin*, the Colorado Book Award winning *Shadow Atlas, What Remains,* and *Sifting the Ashes*, to name a few. She attends the ICFA annually as a guest poet/writer and is a founding member of the Speculative LiteraryFoundation. Instagram: margesimonwrites

Mary Turzillo is a poet and a science-fiction writer. She won the 1999 Nebula award for "Mars Is no Place for Children," and the Science Fiction Poetry Association's 2013 Elgin award for her dark poetry collection, *Lovers & Killers.* With Marge Simon, she won another Elgin, 2015, for *Sweet Poison.* Her most recent book is *Cosmic Cats and Fantastic Furballs,* 2022, short stories about felines of all flavors, from comic to dark, from WordFire Press. You may meet her at Conference on the Fantastic in the Arts, in Orlando, Florida, March 13-16, 2024, where she will be Author Guest of Honor. She is married to award-winning science fiction writer, Geoffrey Landis. She is at work on *Callisto,* a novel combining science fiction with her other passion, fencing. She does enjoy stabbing people, but, no, her bloodlust has not converted her to a vampire. Yet.

Dedications

To Jack, who through darkness sought light.
—Mary Turzillo

To Lisa Mannetti, she left us too soon.
—Marge Simon

Table of Contents

Who Live in Darkness

They live in darkness and they wait, often coming
forth when everything is silent. Sometimes they arrive
in turbulent storms like the one coming now, in high
country. I sit here shivering when I remember what
was done, what they might do—I know no other
recourse. I feel their presence as I watch the aspens
sway. Winds push past me to the valley below, and
night creatures lay low to earth. When I was young, I
did some foolish things, I know only that I remember
their screams. But I never touched a one of their
small bodies, never wrapped them in towels, that
was someone else. Never washed the blood and dirt
from my hands in the river that ran forever down
the Colorado canyon. I see them floating down the
mountainside, eyes blazing with hatred, small white
hands reaching for me. And their laughter blends with
the growing storm, with the realization that this time, I
am their victim.

-Marge Simon

Invisible

Blind fools:
we walk each day
in an unseen death cloud,
not seeing its tendrils invade
our throats.

Walk soft,
wear a white mask
hope it won't choose to take
us, or those we have come to love.
Just hide.

A gift
found at your door
may conceal its poison
or detonate invisibly:
death mist.

It may
wear your friend's face
beware sighs or hand clasps
for someone you think that you know
may kill.

We pray
it will someday
become bored with us prey,
drift to a far away island.
Just pray

-Mary Turzillo

On the Moors

Beasties legends old
demanding retribution,
Satan's Mistress O' the Moors,
and one bloodthirsty Hound.

    Fog forms a ghostly blanket as as we gather for the sacrifice. Maire and Thad bring the lure, a tubercular harlot, her protests stilled by sedatives and gin.The sea winds penetrates our bones as we labor up the slender path, thick with crowberry and moss, all for promise, a glimpse of her, our Goddess of the Moors. Twilight falls, and bitter cold. The musicians set up and begin. As one, we sway to the dirge, Todd's oboe's foreboding notes, the last sad chords of cello, as Jocelyn draws her bow.

When all is still, Raymond makes the whore to lie upon the sacrificial stone. He strips her nude, then splays her legs and ties her down. Our chanting fills the wind. If midnight comes without a sign, we'll have to slice the bitch's throat, and leave her to that Hound.

-Marge Simon

Crawl Space

       When we moved into this house, there was
a woman living walled up, under the first floor
floorboards and the basement ceiling. She said she'd
been there for maybe fifteen years--hid there in the
crawl space as a fifth grader, a runaway, scared to go
to school without her English homework. Can you
imagine what an ogre that teacher was?
       Former tenant told us he heard the screams,
but he was scared, so he just fed her bread and canned
soup. She says her last name's Martin, pretty common,
hard to trace. Parents probably moved. We decided
it would cause too much hoopla to let her out. They'd
probably investigate, make it a crime scene, try to make
us leave, and it's a nice house. We give her leftovers,
clothes, and an iPod, though I'm not sure she can read,
and may be blind after that untreated pinkeye a few
months after we moved in. Whatcha going to do?
My cats like to play with her, and now my idiot son
is getting ideas. Oh well. She can't get pregnant, can
she?

-Mary Turzillo

Knock on Wood

I return to the house of my youth, where the Newel
post still stands at the foot of the stairs. Dear memories
of childhood, that staircase with its banister, the game
of Knock-on Wood. Down and around we children
used to slide. At the landing, knock on wood, then
change directions, plunging onward shrieking to the
very bottom stair. There, we'd touch wood once more
at the Newel post, then scramble up to do it all again.
The fastest one would take the win, such a lark in
bygone days!

All too well, I remember Cousin James, who
too often won the game. How he'd crow about his
win, until the day I'd had enough, and pushed him
downstairs to his death. I tell myself I'd meant no
harm; it was just a game gone wrong. I go to leave, but
a whuff of chill air stops me in my tracks. Suddenly
afraid, I turn to see that Newel post knows otherwise, a
fiendish leer within its carved design. My heart thuds!
After all these years, the devil to pay.

-Marge Simon

Little Brother, Big Sis

Wouldn't you love to come out and play?
You have lots of dollies and toys
The ones I left behind, big sis,
Too girlish for young little boys.

I may not be good at badminton, sis
because of not having hands
nor body, nor feet, nor head, sis.
I won't interfere with your plans.

But we can play house or wedding, sis:
In the church by the graveyard lane
I'll be the baby or groom, sis,
Whichever, I'll never complain.

Remember me, sister? Though I'm long lost
Mom says mention me in your prayers
No, do not forget the little dear one,
The brother you threw down the stairs.

-Mary Turzillo

Under a Dark Moon's Horn

Jenna arranges a set of Edwardian chairs side by side on the beach, one red, one brown. I smile, for she wears her best bombazine blouse, giving us a hint of the night's festivities ahead. We bleed ourselves under the dark moon's horn. Jenna's fluted silver dipper shines with our fluids, as smiling, she ladles our offerings into the tureen. Once a communal bowl, it is again so.

Later, when the moon lowers in the southern skies, she summons her warriors to drink. We do enjoy those moments, waiting for another war to manifest itself, if not in the worlds beyond our door, then here. Yes, here on this silver beach, as the goddess known as Jenna plays her cello, Bach's Suite Number Two in D Minor, and the soldiers dance around her, mad with lust.

-Marge Simon

We Must Be

Are we God's pets?
Or marionettes?
Satan's chess pieces on an infinite board?
Toys on a blasted playground?

Who is listening?
Are the old gods behind the curtain?

Ghosts in a drunken machine,
pixels in a cloud,
spinning infinite short circuits?

If we are pets,
we suffer, God smiles:
pain, in truth, is all an illusion.
And when we give up,
exhausted, for a last trip to the vet
on that bridge past a grinning toll-taker,
through rainbows of bathos or horror,
we may find a blanket of nothing
or joy
or a way to discover
how long is the path to forever.

-Mary Turzillo

An American Gothic
-after Grant Wood

A farmer stands, pitchfork in hand, straight and
stoic. Unblinking, he stares at the neighboring farm for
a long time. It belongs to the man who shot his hound
for trespassing. His daughter steps out of the white
frame house to water her geraniums. She notices he
hasn't moved from the spot she last saw him. Worried,
she comes over to touch his shoulder, a question in
her eyes. She tries to see what he's thinking. She tries
to know what he's seen. A garnet ichor slides down
the tines of his pitchfork, drips down his sleeve. If she
notices, she says nothing. She takes his arm and leads
him inside. She wipes the tines and places the fork next
to the door. He never tells her what he has done. But
in the morning, she finds plenty of meat in the freezer,
enough to tide them through till harvest time.

-Marge Simon

Vicious Trees

Not the kind that menace with branches
in Baal's-breath weather,

nor that worm their roots
into your drainage system, flooding your bed,

these trees anaesthetize you with their blossom's scent,
then grow fast enough to wrap twigs around your neck
so in the morning your wife finds your corpse yoked
and strangled,

or they prick you with paralyzing sap
and grow thorns (overnight)
into your belly and eyes,

trees that moan, take pity, take pity,
then turn into dryads and quicken your daughter,
making her mother to logs and oak benches,

or they whisper, just whisper,
how you should leave the forest to them,
how you should just die.

-Mary Turzillo

Hopper's "Nighthawks"

A call on voicemail, six years overdue. He knows
her voice "Let's get together Saturday. Make it after
10pm. That corner diner–our diner, remember?" He
takes a Greyhound to Penn Station. New York blocks
seemed long. He walks seventeen of them. Diner is
all lit up like Christmas and she's sitting with a man
at the counter. When he enters, the guy hastily gets
up and leaves. She flashes him a big smile. "So hey,
Georgie-boy, give us a hug!" He sits. "Who was that
guy?" She ignores him, digs out something from her
purse. "See, Georgie? I saved it all these years. It's very
sweet, really." She unfolds a faded square, pressing it
down flat. The handwriting is his own. He picks up
the letter. "I found it the other day, thought we could
have a laugh," she says, lighting a cigarette. He asks
again, "Who was that – your boyfriend or your john?"
She inhales, shrugs. "He's nobody, Georgie. I thought
we could talk about the fun we used to have, okay? Got
any money? We could --" He stares at her, shaking his
head. "Six years, I waited for you to call. So finally, it
happens. I ride a hundred miles to get here -- and all
you do is play me for a fool. Just like old times, eh?"
She starts to laugh and he slaps her. Caught off-guard,
she falls backward off the stool. Blood begins seeping
from the side of her head. He watches it pool and
spread on the checkered tile.

-Marge Simon

People in the Sun
As Told by a Ghost of the Artist's Model
After Edward Hopper's "People in the Sun"

Here I am posed in the crowd. Do you see? We're
supposed to be tourists gathered to relax and stare at
distant mountains. It's as if the artist were replaying
a silent film of a family vacation. Normally, visitors
here get this explanation: 'The canvas may reflect
Hopper's discomfort in the West, where he found
himself unable to paint with his usual enthusiasm
when confronted by the harsh light and monumental
wonder of the landscape.

I'm that fellow reading in the back row. My wife
Lucia is the woman in the floppy hat. Of course, that's
not a real mountain range on the right. It was actually
just a pile of lights and equipment, so it wasn't difficult
to look bored or unimpressed – just what Hopper
was after, as a fact. I think he was making a statement
about how tourists often miss the awe of the place
they are visiting. Whatever, the scene marks our fifth
anniversary, the last day of our connubial bliss. We
started arguing on the way home and she shot me with
the pretty little handgun I'd given her as an anniversary
gift. It was for her protection, what a laugh! To think,
we'd planned a visit to the Tetons to celebrate. A
shame, all that monumental wonder we missed.

-Marge Simon

"Pray undo this button"

They caught him wandering in the dark
in the Walmart parking lot, in the rain,
with no shoes and a wrong-buttoned shirt:
macular degeneration joins Alzheimer's
and I am not even his fool.

But he needs somebody--anybody--
to take him to the geriatrician.

In the doctor's office,
fingers gone stupid at ninety,
he instructs the nurse,
"I've brought Cordelia with me.
She knows how to undo these buttons.
And no, she's not dead.
How could you say that?"

-Mary Turzillo

Nighthawks
After Edward Hopper's "Nighthawks"

It will seem distant and sweet
calling you with warm light
from the winter rain and long dark.

And when you draw near
you will pause, thinking perhaps music
or is that the odor of baked apples?

But no: there is just humane light
all alone in the dark
waiting and waiting alone.

The door will be unlatched
you will push into the kindly room
where the fire is dying

a room full of shadow.
You remember the light
was from an upper window,

but there is no music
no sound of footfalls
certainly not the sound of breathing

but you know
you are not alone
in this room where you belong/don't belong.

On the desk
rests a letter, half-finished
in a hand you remember,
Is the letter to you?
Is it to Dear Left Behind?
Is it --

14

There is someone upstairs
some one you love
who died long ago

and you will climb.

-Mary Turzillo

The Color Purple

"I collect artists," she says.

She wants three of me. One for the bedroom, one to
tease and one to be nice to her vacuous friends. A
crowd of flies haunts the drawing room. Brown spots
on peaches. A room of scorched music and uncommon
speech.

She admits she chose me for my smile and my purple
tie. "A rich woman always bends toward a creative
man," she says. I grip the champagne flute too tightly.
"Poor you," she says, ministering to my wound with
tweezers and a handkerchief of tears.

The skin around her eyes like cracks in Wedgewood
china. So many lifts and still she's down. She thinks
that someday I'll paint her in the nude, careful to erase
the years. It kills me how she loves to show me off.
Another cocktail afternoon swatting flies. She loves
that part too. "Sarcasm is your style," she says.

She insists that we do it her way. Champagne and
candles. A rosebud curtained bed. All is orchestrated
except me. A thing in her life that doesn't quite work,
doesn't fit, though she seems oblivious to that fact.
Tonight, however, things will go a bit differently than
she plans. I have obtained a vial of Aconite. Just a few
drops in her glass …

Our last toast together is indeed memorable, watching
her gasp for air while turning a most exquisite shade of
purple.

-Marge Simon

Artists

I only know
of this delicious journey
that it will end badly.
But I forget when I feel the symphony
of your breath against my cheek.

See the tree's skeleton,
grace in those brittle angles.
The gnarledness singing
a Picasso, a Dali,
calm minotauromachy
near the end

or the plié of a brown leaf
swooped up just before landing
eventually
turning to mulch,

or the dark redness of the sun, swelling,
knowing it's dying,
taking Jupiter and us with it.

In beauty
take my hand.

-Mary Turzillo

Two Wives

Dr. Jackal had two wives,
both of whom displeased him deeply,
by clawing at each other's eyes
complaining screechily.

Dr. Jackal made a potion,
fed it to the nasty wives.
As cats, except for Friday evenings
They spent their remaining lives.

Bet and Esme spoke in Cattish
of their mutual grievances
and formed a plan to hijack Jackal
and redress their sad mischances.

They drugged poor J. and stole his books
in which they found his formulations
for turning men to unicorns
or dogs, or lizards, or cetaceans.

Dr. Jackal came awake
feeling angry and hungover.
"Pox on these wives," he told himself
"I should instead have took a lover."

Bette and Esme, cowards both
fled to corners most expedient.
But first off, into Jackal's draught
Bette dumped a stray ingredient.

Quite absent-mindedly J. reached
for Jackal's Sovereign Remedy
for Aching Head and Foul Composure,
sold in the states and Canadee,

The extra powder Bette added
was quite by chance a hormone which
added weight and height to birds
and changed the Doctor to an ostrich.

Now Jackal-bird and lady cats
chase each other through the lab
until exhaustion every evening
stops exchange of beak-claw stab.

Jackal-ostrich wishes deeply
he'd never married two proud cats,
while Bette and Esme search his books
for clues on turning birds to rats.

-Mary Turzillo

Medina of the Purple Flames

She comes when you are ready
to accept that which you wish,
the answer to your last dream,
the one that you ran from
all your days. She comes
in the moments before
waking, before you can
rub the dark away, or turn
off your alarm. She comes
soft robed in purple flames,
sweet as some familiar fantasy
you never could remember,
sings you back to forever sleep
in the coils of her dark hair.

-Marge Simon

Visions in a Block of Ice

In dawn's early mist, a woman in a doorway nurses
her child and sneers as we march past her building.
She isn't supposed to do this. We are soldiers, men of
honor, she should be kneeling. When she spits at me, I
fire my torch. Her eyes widen and she screams.

We're told the end is painless, freezing on the spot,
but I have doubts, as it takes   ten long minutes for the
chill to reach her heart. When it's done, the edges of
her dark hair glisten, Escher-patterned crystals dance
in her spectral eyes. The guards come with tongs to
place her in the transport van. But first, with pick and
hammer, her husband removes the tiny babe. Even
in death she may hold it no more, for she has sinned.
Her body will be taken to the temple where relatives
shall pay respects. Though it is unclear to the villagers
why she was shot, they will be allowed to dance and
celebrate the dead. A pity, they enjoy so few occasions.

-Marge Simon

Exorcism

The demons that tormented Samuel moved out
repelled by pills, electrodes, reason's voice
and he shed his exorcism rags, walked into sunlight
did a dance, considered falling in love.
Then he wrote a poem.
Everybody understood this poem, about love,
life, happiness, this coherent, smiling poem.

But where was the damned maelstrom of words,
the forever torrent like a solar storm
or the accretion disk of a black hole
roaring on forever, ripping and snarling
teething on the gristle of my heart, flowing
like matter into the end of the universe?

The new poem, rational and sunny and loved no doubt
by Jesus, hadn't the old
you know madness
say it MADNESS
that Sam rode down to death,
a man clutching a broken beam
riding God's own hurricane.

Sam's happy. Nobody misses a thing.
The demons moved out
stealing Sam's best furniture.

-Mary Turzillo

Ripper Street

Softly settles East End fog, thick with industry's
residue. It leaves an oily coat on the skin, plays games
with the vision. Forms appear and vanish in the mist,
the stink of piss and rotten meat, slimy creatures of
dark alleyways. These streets, the Ripper's playground.

Me being young, and with no binding ties, I once
went slumming with the lads. Begging favors of Miss
Mary, we taking turns with her to satisfy our bursting
loins. And that she did with competence, such was
her service for our coins. When we were done, we
bade good night and off she went into that dense
Whitechapel fog.

Years passed, and I'm a doctor now, with a different
take on whores. They're still corrupting honest men,
giving them most dreadful maladies. I should know,
being one among them on that certain night. Now I
walk these midnight streets alone, carrying my own
assorted tools. There's many a strumpet up ahead, for a
trained man skillful with the blade.

-Marge Simon

Solstice

your voice on a cell phone
you have left your car by the side of a road
I am on an ice-slick road in the dark
woods to either side
sometimes a frozen pond
or a flash of light from a deserted mill

you are wandering in the woods, lost
you have left your car
and you have no coat, hat, gloves
wandering in your moccasins
your feet soaked, snow falling on your hair

I drive scared on the two-lane road
beyond the county line
there are no other tracks in the snow but mine
your tire tracks are covered
as the snow falls harder now
as it turns to sleet

and your cell phone no longer answers
I fear that you lost it, too

please, answer, please call me
I will find you and take you
where it is warm, where there are Christmas lights
where there is hot tea and food
where we can find your medicine

and I think, here, you are here
just a few dozen paces from the road
in the woods, in the tangle of darkness
in the sleet, and I stop, I open my car door
I have a warm coat and I get out
and begin to search
forgetting my gloves.

-Mary Turzillo

The Boyfriend

"But how will I know that you love me more than you
do your wife?" she asks. "Prove it! He grins. "You
want proof?" He pulls her photo from his wallet, flips
his lighter. She watches as that pretty face blackens
and falls away. It isn't entirely destroyed; she can still
see the eyes. She rends the piece with her dinner fork.
Swirls the ashes.

One day, he takes her to his house out in the boonies.
Her father had given the newlyweds a one bedroom
on a bit of dry prairie land. The bedroom has a crib
in one corner. His wife is at work, their baby is with
her mother. A few months later, when she's pregnant
with his child, he's gone. She remembers those eyes,
wonders how many photos of his wife he'll be burning
in years to come.

She returns to the homestead where his wife cares
for her little one. In her arms, she carries her own
infant. The wife looks at the newborn. The wife's
baby and the newborn in its mother's arms on her
doorstep could be twins, so much do they resemble
their father. "Come on in," says the wife. After a
few exchanges, the wife takes down a photo of their
unfaithful, cheating husband/lover. And, each holding
a corner, they set the portrait aflame.

-Marge Simon & Mary Turzillo

A Gentlewoman to Save a Fallen Angel

My father, a taxidermist, died when I was little more than a child. His shop was left to my skinflint paternal grandfather, who never fancied me. Called me the devil's spawn, none of his dear son's. He cast me into the street, and I made my way as best I could. I soon learned much of the courtesan's art, including the sponge to kill the serum that lights babies in a woman's womb. But it failed, and now I am burdened to provide not just for myself but for a babe in--what? five months?

I live in dread of the Ripper, so I choose my corner and my customers with care. But nobody comes on this dark night, except this prissy gentlewoman, garbed all in black, veil and all. And she takes my hand, says to me, "Poor child, you must sin more. Come with me to a haven for you and your sisters in sin." I try to shake her off--she is scaring away my usual gentlemen.

But she embraces me and says, "Dear one, pray with me. There is hope." And in a secret voice, "I can rid you of that little one in your belly." And I am tempted. "Come with me, my poor fallen angel." Leading me to a deserted place by the docks. "Lie down." I resist, but she kisses my cheek and I smell something--is it lilacs, or paraffin? The bed is soft and clean, and I am so tired. She presses the scented cloth to my face, and I nod. But then I hear the snick of a switchblade, and I am blazingly awake.

She is strong, and in the battle I feel hardness under her skirt. I place a hot hand on it, as if to caress, and she falters. I wrestle the blade from her and plunge it into her eye, again and again. When she is well dead, I feel again for the hardness. I cut. But what now?

This place is private, and I remember what my father taught me of his art. Tools? I could steal them from the taxidermy shop. No time to do it properly. Daylight reveals him/her standing propped on a shed near the dock. Only as an afterthought do I take the sterling I find in his/her reticule.

-Mary Turzillo

Among the Ruins

She walks among the ruins of Central Quarters,
once a hospice for the Third War Refugees
now a bombed-out wreckage of fallen stone,
a sad and broken testament to time.

There is no safe place now for the living.
Would there were, she'd not be starving,
the craving for blood is now intolerable,
all the scavengers are gone, even the rats.

She remembers a life before this craving,
a lover with sad brown eyes and yellow hair,
hands that spanned two of hers, the feel
of his warm breath and her arousal.

Sometimes she wonders where he is,
if he is still alive –and glad she doesn't know,
because he would not be safe from her lust,
the need is so strong, it clouds her mind.

Nightfall and the skies shed moonlit drops,
crystalline on the white marble stones
as if to show her a path where there's none.
Such deceit, she mutters to herself.

A wind rises and she senses someone
padding softly though the shadows
There is the smell of blood, but it is old,
as the smell of a dry leaf smells old.

She turns as he steps out from the shadows,
a man with pale blond hair and smiling.
His eyes reflect his skin, a certain nutmeg brown,
yet his familiar face is marked with sadness.

Suddenly she knows – indeed, they both know –
they and their undead kindred are the only creatures left.
There is no life-blood to be had. Only their own.

-Marge Simon

The Human Guest

The mating time was brief this year.
Our women sang notes like
floss on the wine-wind plains.

A human came who forced his seed
on Ala of the Yellow Eyes. We pretended
to be honored; we felt otherwise.

Afterward, our Ala changed.
She cut her marvelous hair,
which had shined so dark and long
grown down below her waist.

She wandered off to the Darklands,
heavy with child and none to celebrate.
We mourn her fate. If she survives,
she'll raise his spawn alone.

She was the envy of us all.
When the child is born,
she'll burn his father's image
in the sands of our dead oceans.

The human sits on our sacred stones.
He preens his beard and leers at females,
with no more thoughts to waste on Ala;
he never even knew her name.

Come burrow season, we prepare,
sharpen our talons on caddo root.
When the freezing gales begin,
the human will demand sanctuary,
as his kind always does.

We will confirm his welcome
with the strewing of his bones.

-Marge Simon

Blood Sisters

Thanks for the light, lover. Come close, I shall tell you
a secret about me and my sisters. Tonight, you may
call me Carmilla. Born of landed gentry, a life of leisure
lay ahead until I was courted by a certain Count. You
might say he gave my death – er, life, new meaning. By
mutual consent, we enjoy an open union.

My closest sister, sweet Aimee, traveled from Paris
to the Colonies in 1868. She settled in postbellum
New Orleans and became a respectable mistress, and
later, an elite Madam. Adventurous Delphine took
off for the Libyan Desert, hoping to sample Rommel's
blood in '41. Sometimes we see her face depicted on
the floors of bars in Cairo where various pleasures
may be procured. Miriam left for Bangladesh in '63.
She was the religious one, though meditation didn't
work for her. Still, she likes that filthy place, perhaps
for its music, but more likely for the ease of sanguine
samples. Ling is the oldest of us all, certainly the most
talented as well. She pens songs for rock stars, assists
in their success or failure depending on her inscrutable
mood.

Many years have passed since we were turned, yet our
faces are ageless. Though the wine is better quality,
the blood is thinner. Manhattan's neon lights form
irreal colors, incredible as our own undead lives. New
Year's Eve we gather to watch traffic from my flat, dots
moving along the horizon like a zircon necklace. We
toast the new year, for tomorrow promises passions we
have yet to know.

-Marge Simon

I Have Drunk

I have drunk the blood of virgins
yet been but faintly aroused, by no means sated.

I have drunk the blood of sages and men of science
and am no wiser for its salt tang.

I have drunk the blood of cows and pigs
and it tasted no more degrading than more noble
fluids.

I have drunk the blood of werewolves
and stand unchanged, strong, without rage or
brutality.

I have drunk the blood of dragons
and it burned through my body
leaving my mouth scorched and my pores scalded.

I have drunk the blood of gods--
Dionynus, Aphrodite, even your Jesus
and I am still mortal
and still I thirst.

-Mary Turzillo

Haiku

I tread rose petals
crushed to wet pulp
walking away

-Mary Turzillo

The Weather in Belize

Sometimes the soldier sees in perpetuity the memory
of a lover. He returns to it again and again, something
that can't be soiled by words, even those in confidence
a moment or so. For one hour of the waking afternoon,
stretching the silence, the heartbeat music of heat and
sweat. He knows she will not come to him today.

Downstairs in the foyer embraced by statues of dead
generals with their hollow-eyes and dour mouths, a
voice hangs in the gum thick air. "Hello, lover." In
a moment that lasts an eon, slips off her clothes and
with warm hair and mouth folds in on Father Riley,
touching him tenderly as if his skin were bloodied
from a flogging, as if his mind were numb. He doesn't
see the blade of her silver knife, doesn't feel it slit his
throat.

In the cool shadows of her chambers, Commander
Cassia, head of militia on New Earth, fondles her
partner's breasts, contemplating new war games to
play with her soldiers, lest they grow indolent in the
sleepy afternoons.

-Marge Simon

Pangs

Breathe woman, breathe
if you get tired, sleep between contractions
regular, until the man with the blade comes
and zips out your child.

They clean the blood, ready to stitch your wound,
lift out the blood and flesh.

Press your face to his small belly
listen to him laugh.

sleep when the baby sleeps

And your child grows and grows sad
and zips himself out,
out of the world
his body too heavy.

They slice the Y wound
look for the reason he died
lift out the mass of blood and flesh.

Press your face to the ground
listen to silence and worms

and you have deathpangs.
Breathe breathe between the pangs
resisting all anodynes, resisting,
not wanting to let him go,

bearing him like a sword into memory.

-Mary Turzillo

Ivan and the Goddess of Time

After dinner, Ivan is out for a smoke, as he's wont to do if weather permits. The oaks are limed in shadows, the heavens ablaze with points of light. This night seems different, full of portent. He strikes a match to his pipe, wondering if he might discover some new constellation of his own invention. But the flame goes out as a woman materializes, the sexiest young woman he's ever seen. She appears to float his way, holding an object lit with an otherworldly glow. Ivan stares with pipe unlit, wondering where she comes from, and why here, to his back yard.

"I come to share," she says, revealing a golden hour glass, its top half almost empty. Trembling, Ivan touches it. "I know who you are, gorgeous. You're an angel, come to tell me that my time here is at an end." His eyes narrow, "Is this not so?"

"Wrong, Ivan! I'm no angel, I'm the Goddess of Time. As to why I'm here—oh!"
Ivan instantly snatches the glass out of her hand, turning it back over as he does. "Say no more, you beautiful broad. I get to live as long as I want, now. With another lifetime ahead, I can prepare myself to be president of our nation. I can have all the sexy women I wish, starting with you."

The goddess begins laughing. "Do you actually believe I'd bring you my sacred Glass of Hours? I have a bet with the God of Fools that you'd do something like this. He thought you'd beg me for a kiss, maybe ask me to sleep with you. Hah!"

"I was just about to propose both of those things," says Ivan. "But you are saying this is a fake?"

"It surely is, but you're smarter than I'd thought, Ivan. Anyway, it doesn't matter now." Ivan stares speechless as the lovely goddess unhinges her jaw. "It gets boring, being a Goddess. Sometimes I need a change of pace. I'm moonlighting as a vampire this evening, that's what I wanted to share, little man."

-Marge Simon

Frida's Bomb

We toured California when we married. That was before the Great Quake, before the bomb that caused it. The bomb that your father insisted came from South America, and you'd agreed with him. He said it was that "pinko feminist radical" Frida Kahlo's doing. He'd read something about her in a magazine years ago. Didn't even know who the woman really was or when she lived. But neither did you, my bride. Anyway, whether bomb or quake, California is an island to itself now, and we can't go there for our anniversary. If that ever gets here. In fact, don't plan on it. I am tired of arguing about what really happened. Tired of you, tired of being always hungry and thirsty, tired of breathing ash filled air, walking along the Nevada coast for days without a bath. If we keep walking, maybe we'll reach South America and find sanctuary. But who are we kidding? Maybe it is all Frida Kahlo's fault. She with her exotic birds, her strange flowers. Those accusing eyes. Those darkly burning eyes.

-Marge Simon

Eel Soup

So, the time has come. He can't stand watching her suffer any longer.

He prepares their last meal from scratch. He has procured the vegetables from the neighbor's garden. The onions are still good, as well, the carrots and potatoes. A can of stewed tomatoes, peppercorns and salt, these are in the cabinet. The most important ingredient of all -- the eels, he has obtained at the docks early this morning. He is careful to add them with their blood as the soup cools. They are finely chopped and raw, camouflaged with cabbage leaves. A modified and deadly vichyssoise served in her shining silver tureen.

He wheels her chair to the table. She's so frail now, her skin almost transparent. The plague that sweeps the world hasn't touched him as yet. Perhaps he is one of the few that are resistant. He frowns at the irony. His own life isn't worth bothering with – but hers is another story. Such talents she has, so much to look forward to! Her paintings were selling well. She had begun composing music to accompany the presentations in galleries. She called it "bonding kinetic transitions." But no more -- this strain of the virus knows no prejudice.

He picks up a photograph of them when they were young, remembers the smell of her wool coat, the way her mouth chokes back a laugh in the photo. She'd loved his jokes – even the lame ones. Then came a time when laughter stopped. Like the sound of her voice, a bare whisper now.

Once she'd said his dreams were all smashed up inside. "Gray on gray. Form without substance," she said. She was the artist. She had dreams for both of them. They are silent during dinner. He offers her another helping. To his surprise, she nods with a lopsided smile. She knows. He turns away to wipe his eyes. After dinner, he helps her out of the wheelchair, lays her gently on the bed. The muscle cramping will begin soon, ending the beating of her heart.

But instead of closing her eyes and lying back, she pushes herself up. "Hand me that novel you were reading to me last night, sweetheart. I am feeling so much better, I should like to find out how it ends myself." He is stunned. This is the first time she's said entire sentences in many days. And wanting to read? How can this be -- the eels have cured the virus? Her eyes are bright and her pulse steady. There's a healthy flush to her cheeks that wasn't there before dinner.

As he hands her the book, he feels a sharp pain in his stomach as the cramps begin. With a terrible chill, he remembers it was to be their last meal.

-Marge Simon

Duel in the Dark

The woman is told not to come,
but how could she not?

They bring seconds,
at midnight, not dawn,
and each bears a lantern
in his off-hand, in both cases, left.

The referee says "Fence!"
and they rush forward,
clash, lunge, parry,
counter-parry, then, nobody hit yet,
step back, glowering,
in flickering yellow light.

Again: one flèches arrow-swift,
the other spins, lunges at his back
but: draws no blood,
and the duel continues.

A third flurry of blades --
and the husband, who challenged,
drops his lantern.
It flares out.

His second rushes forward, but there is no flint, no
match, no flame.
The lover, the challenged,
begs to give a light.
but the challenger says no.
After all, if he carries no light
he is harder to see
harder to hit.

Dishonorable! says the challenged.
But the referee says: Continue!

The younger man hurtles forward,
misses, stumbles,
narrowly avoids the stroke to the heart.
Stands, trembling.
Then blows out his lantern.

And they clash in the dark.

At dawn
the referee gone:
two are dead, and two fled.

And the woman alleges she never was there,
those seconds were friends of her husband
and of his rival. No one she knew.

She sits alone
her lantern dark and cold.

-Mary Turzillo

The Hat

Bathed in blood and fire and hate
faithful to all things red,
the citizen's hat fits snugly,
as if knitted just for you.

When you can stand the pain no longer,
you claw it from your hair in shreds,
ensuring no one else could wear the thing,
fearing its terrible powers.

How could you know it would
emerge with a morsel of your mind
and thrive and grow much larger,
until it was indeed another hat.

Yesterday you saw it on someone
walking briskly down the street
with an AKA slung across his back,
eyes full of blood and fire,
      and hate.

-Marge Simon & Mary Turzillo

The Vampire Ball

Tonight, a celebration such as Machiavelli himself might have planned, with elite victims of high social standing. Dashing and dapper, the Monsignor descends the stairs, flourishing a polished cane. The shine on his shoes would put the moon to shame. Midway, he readjusts his ascot, sets the brim of his top hat at a jaunty angle. Maurice, his faithful Grenville, bows low to present his Master's chosen escort, Ramona of the raven locks. She wears a low-cut dress to match his tie. How the lady trembles, half-paralyzed with fear, her long, pale neck at his command! Once, a woman of her class would have scorned his presence, before he joined the ranks of the Undead. He may well take his vengeance now, for Ramona knows her lover hangs by his ankles in the Pit of the Pendulum below stairs. Distressed, she begs him for mercy, but he flashes her a smile, "Please me, and your man may be spared."

Among their many talents, it is no secret that vampires know how to party. Locked in waltz position, they begin to dance with tiny nips, like kisses on their partner's necks. Much like a punch bowl, they take in more as the night progresses. Graceful movements continue to the music, orchestrated with attention to the draining of the blood. Come dawn, they leave in drunken disarray –all but Monsignor. A soft rain has begun falling when his coach returns. He carries fair Ramona in his arms. The Pendulum has long been done; chunks of scattered skin and bone, bloody pools on the basement floor. Holding her head to witness this, he drains her dry. Typically, he's saved the best for last.

-Marge Simon

Diana and Guinevere

"Ah, Guinevere," she sighed, "Men are animals. Some
are foxes, some bulls, some jackals, some are of the
reptile family. All
are lower creatures, sleek and enticing in cases, but
low.

"Dear Diana!" I answered. "True, but there is love;
what can we say of it?"

"Oh," she said, shifting her weight on the blue silk
cushion (in scorn),
"Let us admit we are low creatures too. Observe the
barnyard duckling
imprinted on its mother duck. Or on the barn cat. Or
on a goose, or a mongrel."

"I have been so imprinted," I cried.
"What pain! The fool knows his power and uses it. Or
slinks, embarassed,
like a dog caught chasing chickens."

We sat, silent, tragic-eyed, drinking gen mai cha.

Diana considered, shaking the folds of her heavy silk
gown,
blue shadows in a blue shimmer.

"It is no less ordinary than the common cold," she told
me.
"And no more curable." I replied, "Do you count
yourself immune?"
"Ah, no! Dear Guinevere, I have loved toads and
snakes, dogs and roosters,
low things, even spiders, if you count them as men."

42

Just then Lancelot, her lover, passed below, beating his brow,
reading a letter, smothering a sob.

I swore I recognized her scented paper, and her elaborate script.

-Mary Turzillo

The Sinner

May the gods forgive me, for I must have sinned.

It began six months ago when I broke out in great welts all over my body. Every pore of my skin was on fire. This wretched condition finally subsided, but then the skin started peeling off my hands and the soles of my feet.

When I go to work in the fields it is like walking on shards of broken glass. I must not think of that. I have my duties. I am expected to finish all before I may rest. Last night, I stole a pair gloves to keep from shredding my own flesh.

The peeling continues all over my body where the rash was. The new layers on my hands and feet are bright and tender. But it is not a normal color – not the color of our people, and that bothers me. I wear the gloves all the time now.

Today a larger strip loosens from my right arm. I pick at it until it lets go. It's most of the diameter of my arm. I fold it up and put it under my mattress. But first, I notice that the new skin is also dark and mottled like that on my palms and feet. It is as if I'm marked, like a child of an Evil God. Perhaps I am paying for the sins of some relative.

I have been over and over it in my head. What did I do? I just do what I'm told. Taking the prisoners out of their barracks at gunpoint and walking them to the fields where each is made to dig his own grave. When one is finished to my satisfaction, I put a bullet in his temple. I am not even in charge of the women and children, so it's not that troublesome.

This day, the last of my old skin peeled off. I have stored it under my mattress as well. The only part that hasn't yet peeled is my face. Still, it is obvious that I am soon to be wholly marked with the same color skin as our sinful enemy. The shame is too great to bear. Come night, I shall gather my old skin into a bundle, for it is indeed the one thing that I truly own and therefore I may dispose of it as I see fit. I shall take the shovel to dig my grave in the fields. I have the pistol. One bullet will suffice.

May the gods forgive me.

-Marge Simon

Legend

*See that ancient piano by the door? Looks like it's been left
it out in the rain for a couple of centuries, right? There's a
story that goes with that old piece of junk. Back at the turn of
the century, it was shiny new, imported from some European
country. Only one person for miles around who could play it
right. Her husband was a drunk, used to beat her, but she'd
get away and come here to play. One night, he followed her
here. He took a baseball bat to that piano, made sure it was
broken beyond repair. After that, she kind of disappeared.
Legend goes her ghost still hangs around. Some claim you
can hear her playing in the darkest hours before dawn.*

The Woman in the Bar
The door swings open. A slender woman stands
there, framed against the sunset.
The bartender knows her. He fixes her a glass of his
best whiskey on the rocks.

She walks over to the piano and plays a few chords.
Her face is as velvety smooth as the white of her hair.
She's old enough to be your mother, but that doesn't
matter.

When she starts playing, everyone shuts up to listen,
even the guy in the booth coughing blood in his beer.

She plays the blues and more. Like more than words
and deep and it goes straight inside all the places
where you've tried to hide your fear,digs them out and
makes you feel all right about it.

She plays as long as she feels like it and then she
stops.

There is another drink waiting for her but she just
leaves it there on the piano.

She glances at you on the way out, a tree of owls in
her eyes.

She's brought you Jasmine candles and dandelion
wine, a first passionate kiss, country walking winter
days.

Maybe it was just your imagination, but if you were
hurting deep inside, or sorrowing over a lost love,
it doesn't matter anymore, she's fixed what was
broken.

-Marge Simon

Heavy Metal

In this dimly lit room,
my mother is dying.
The girl in the other bed needs her hair washed, so
the aides wake her at two AM
and wheel her away
into the dark hospital hall.
Her face is fresh and sweet and amazed.
This can't be right.
I want to tell her parents
that the aides do things their way
that they are treating the child unfeeling
like a dog or a doll.

My mother is dying.
And I hear heavy metal music I can't make out.
Is it from the other side,
the bed where the poor unwashed girl suffers?

When the girl is wheeled to the showers
I try to find the source of the music
but the room is so dark
I can't find the switch for the TV or radio.

Such a fresh-faced girl:
why must she listen to growling and threats?
What happened to the poor thing?
Born challenged? In a car wreck? Failed suicide
attempt?
Is the harsh music her choice?

I know something about heavy metal
but this is not a band I recognize
and my son is not here to advise.

My mother dies.
My mother dies.
My mother dies.

A woman in white says my mother is dead.
And the music stops.
The music was the oxygen
pumped to keep my mother alive
until she stopped by herself.
It was a breathing machine.
It was the rhythm of life, not death.
The metal was heavy indeed.

They wheel the girl back from the bright white
through the dark hall
to her now-single dark room,
her hair wet, her eyes red, wide and confused.
They put her to bed
and there is no more music.

-Mary Turzillo

The Child Remembers

The child remembers: "I watched, but no misty ghost
floated up from his still body."

The child's mother says, "There's no such thing as
ghosts. Where is this dead man you insist looks like
your father?"

The child points to his parents' bedroom.

The child's mother smiles. "That's all right, then. That's
exactly where I left his body."

The child doesn't answer, but now he can see his
father's ghost readying to haunt his mother all the days
of her life. He grins.

– Marge Simon & Mary Turzillo

Easy Prey

Three aunties with alluring smiles -- a photograph
from long ago. A fourth sister is cut from it, most
probably my mother's own, for she did not belong.
Her eyes were too blue, her face too serious, and most
tragic of all, she rejected immortality.

I'm sorry never to have met my kindred temptresses
– back in the day, they performed at their own salon.
The "Gentleman's Guide to Better Houses" did well for
my aunts, and by the same token, a veritable gold mine
for men in need.

For willing patrons, they played many roles, from
Cleopatra to Belle Starr. No man dared complain
about after the performance, when he found himself
in a room of musky perfume after being awakened
by his own screams. There was always the memory of
cold lips upon his neck and the slamming of a door.
Someone in another room would be playing "Aura
Lea" softly on the harmonica. Those were the days!

Today the internet abounds with opportunities to hit
it off with lonely individuals, (but no touching!) such
boring, easy prey.

-Marge Simon

Blue Sky Somewhere

Thea parts the curtains on the day ahead, then quickly ducks away. Sunlight unfurls from the window panes sparkling an unused coffee cup and a basket of imaginary rolls. She knows it's make-believe, a tableau laid out by habit. Useless to pretend she's still human, sequestered within her home, but it is all she's had for centuries.

On the floor, shadows of cherry trees in bloom remind her spring has arrived. How she longed for a glimpse of cobalt sky, a sight she treasured on the shores of Attica. Those sweet days, a memory from centuries ago when she was young, unaware her mortality was soon to change. Yet change it did, thanks to the man with no reflection who made her one of his kind against her will. In recent years, the bloodied smoke of cities bleeds into a wounded sky; the atmosphere so thick with toxic fumes, few mortals dare to walk the streets without a mask. She knows this from the papers.

It seems unfair that she must bear the situation, knowing it was never her intention. But worse, the shrinking population bodes her ultimate demise. She wanders darkened rooms, touching surfaces, feeling the measure of textures, the contrast of cloth and stone, glass and polished wood. Things in her small world she knows so well. Inside things, held dearly but dearer still the feel of sun on skin. A patch of blue sky, there must be a glimpse of it somewhere.

Why wait any longer?

A twist of latch, an open door. She steps into the light.

-Marge Simon

Black Roses

These black roses
are they dead, dear?
or did you dye them
with your own slow bile?
They are a tribute, I know,
because I lie here cold.
But you know something about that
with your shrill songs and appetites.
I love this glade where you have buried me,
though none knows but you,
the shovel carefully washed, and returned
after you heaved earth all day.
And thank you again for the roses,
which, on second thought, seem to be crepe
perhaps cut from your black wedding dress
worn twice -- or was it thrice?
Before and after I went away.

-Mary Turzillo

Sirens

Sirens are thirsty tonight.
In the brine, they lap you like kits,
coyly pretending to be pretty and helpful.
They suck your tears, your spit, the plasma from your
blood.
They reach out tendrils of singing.
You know you need them --
how can you say no?

They work so hard for you,
dragging with the current,
to pull you under,
to kiss you to breathless,
to take your pleasure,
to slap you against the sand.
You can lie there. It's easy.
You will give what they want.
You will bloat in the tide.

When all thirst is satisfied,
the female slaves file out
to tend the bodies awash in the tide.
Sweet and sad, their voices swell in mourning,
that the sailors' journey into the next world
be swift and tempered with kindness,
for all the cruel matter of their passing.
Their bodies are wrapped in clean linen,
buried deep within the island sands.

The Sirens remain silent
until their victims are dispatched,
the last gull with its last morsel,
their slaves again sequestered
in their grotto by the sea.

Then again, those bitches mount the rocks
to play their harps, to weave their spells
into the winds of ill fortune
that speed you luckless sailors by.

-Marge Simon & Mary Turzillo

Haiku

fractal monster
slow eternally branching
That oak

-Mary Turzillo

FAQ

Is death contagious?
Death is transmitted by a spirochete endemic to fresh
peaches, phytoplankton, and dreams of empty houses.

Does death wear a disguise?
Death has a splendid set of polished pewter teeth,
worn only at the decease of royal infants.

*Is it true that a new dessert incorporates sugar, creme
fraiche, and crystallized death? What is the calorie count per
hundred grams?*
You would find that fatiguing.

*Is is polite to hum along if the bereaved bursts into flames?
Should one intervene before the etheric stage?*
Yes, and never.

*I have seen skeins of gray linen draped on bare trees. Are
these sacs of freshly laid death eggs?*
One should not offend the modesty of mothers.

*Might one dance with death at an afternoon tea and still call
oneself holy?*
If decorously clad.

*What is death's favorite beverage? Should bottles of
absinthe be concealed when death visits?*
Absinthe is entirely correct, garnished with fresh
thujone.

Can death estivate in the shells of the fighting conch?
In temperate zones.

*Does death preen before mirrors staged in infinite
regression?*
Wouldn't you?

If death is seen walking on an interstate carrying a leaking
gas can, should one offer assistance?
How could you resist?

Is it true that if you draw four deuces in a row, or if you
fail to promote an eligible pawn, death will slash
your hamstrings?
This is a superstition promoted by Borges cultists and
the Penitentes.

Does death experience orgasm?
Only if you like.

Am I going to die?
No.

Is anybody I know going to die?
Only persons you know very remotely. Your touch
confers immunity.

Does the thicket conceal death better at dawn or dusk?
Both.

Does death have a favorite number?
Yes.

Does death have a home town? A native language? A
weakness for leibfraumilch?
Yes.

Will I know to close my eyes?
Yes. Yes.

Yes

-Mary Turzillo

In the Dark House

Bathed in blood and fire
you were pledged to all things red.
The spider that crawled up your nose
emerges with a morsel of your soul,
a fat drop of blood
in the dark house
like a copper coin

-Mary Turzillo

Honors for My Lovers

Summer has fled. It is the dying season, when
multiple graves beyond the house must be tended.
I begin with arrangements of chrysanthemums and
hyacinths, some more bountiful than others. A wreath
for Rusty, who smelled of smoke and gasoline, his
kisses drove me wild. Then Michael, strong as stone,
with a smile that made me melt. Alas, our grunts
and moans were hardly meant to last. A vase for pale
haired Lars, with ice blue eyes and honeyed breath.
The two of us in flagrante delicto, photos taken by
his wife's detective sadly ended our affair. But sweet
Samuel was a needy man, caring for his mother twenty
years until her death. My dearest, always ready to shed
tears whatever the performance, whatever the book.
For his bones, a garland of my best wisteria. Tonight,
I light three candles, one for each who shared my bed,
excepting Samuel. A kiss before dreamtime, for Sam's
head rests stately on the pillow next to mine.

-Marge Simon

Ailurophobe

Ailurophobe.
And yet.
This sleek gray velvet beast,
Warm like a baguette fresh from the oven.

Eat me.

It settles on her throat.
She is sleeping.
The beast, a she cat, purrs soft, unending thunder.

The ailurophobe squirms, restive.
The beast's tail insinuates around her neck
Its breath simmers in her mouth.

Wake up! Danger!
Moisture, a hot drug, blooms between her legs
She moans, undulates, hypnogogically ignited.

The beast drills her eyes with its own slit pupils.
Glamorous eyes!
Spread your legs, my dear.

The beast grows longer, woman-size now,
to mimick the ailurophobe.
The beast grows breasts, firm, nipples pink as its nose.
But the beast's hands still sport claws.
And those hands caress with tiny prickles
rousing the ailurophobe to urgency.
The ailurophobe bucks against the beast.

Urgent, urgent, please let me--
And climaxes.
It is done.
The beast shrinks, says one final meow
The meow is not "I love you," but

Just "Finished with you now."

The ailurophobe wakes, fully.
Sheets drenched in body-dew and vaginal oozings.

She looks at her hands. The backs begin to fur.
She is shrinking.
The size of a prey animal.
Her hands
have claws.

And starting again, the fear, the longing.

-Mary Turzillo

The Book Club Meeting

The ice has melted on the walk, green blossoms emerge on stark branches; winter's turn is done. It is the second Wednesday of the month, the Book Club meeting is at hand. At the door, a gray cat waits, tail curled around his paws.

By twos and threes, they arrive. They all so love these gatherings. A stack of books awaits discussion. On a shelf, the shiny silver coffee pot, with cups and cream. They help themselves. The worn carpet is stained from Solstice rituals. Blood on blue turns garnet over time, but no one seems to mind. It enhances the nostalgia.

The tabby weaves in and out between trouser legs and skirts, rests on laps for strokes by bone-thin hands. Today it is Mary Shelley's best seller. They love to debate the technicalities. Tim Watkins insists she couldn't have written it without a man's help. Several ladies laugh him down. "Next month, we must invite the author, wouldn't that be fun?", says Tilly Oster. She sits, pleased that all agree.

When the old Grandfather Clock strikes five, they celebrate the newly dead -- Old Hiram with dimpled cheeks laid to rest with his black-haired bride, and sweet Jezebel, who'd fed the ravens during winter. Given time, they might attend.

The moon begins its tour across the early evening skies, it's time to leave. Beyond the porch, the members fade into the night. The room is darkly barren, save for the silken tabby, purring softly on a parlor chair.

-Marge Simon

Oblivio Mori

Try to ignore the bellows of steers that die so you can
          dine,
children killed helping their leader
kill a different set of children.
Think about it when the spirit wind
drives bitter from the north
and forget it when the cat falls asleep in your lap,
when you taste veal marsala swimming in cream.
Forget, for whole days at a time,
when Indian summer beats your heart like a satin
          drum,
that you are condemned too.

The cat knows about death as somebody going away,
maybe another cat, or the aging owner,
but not its own end.
The panther knows about death as a mouthful of blood
the wildebeast's throat, the jaw's sweetness,
and maybe dimly senses if it is not careful, the bullet,
but to her, death is bright and immediate, or never.

Knowing is the original sin.
The Eden curse you didn't need;
you were already under the stone lid of Think Ahead.

Your only salvation is forgetting or denying, or planning
to sidestep the virus, the rival, the gunshot, the blade,
the tumor, the god-in-a-box.
Immorality comes in ten minute hunks,
ten blessed minutes, like the cat in your lap.

Mary Turzillo

Acknowledgements

MARGE SIMON:

Previously Published:

"Vision in a Block of Ice", *Space & Time*, 2020
"Eel Soup", *Space & Time*, 2010
"Nighthawks" " *What Remains*, 2022
"Ripper Street" *Pen of the Damned*, August 24, 2022
"Among the Ruins," *Illumen*, 2019
"Blood Sisters" *Night to Dawn*, 2023
"The Vampire Ball", *Night to Dawn*, 2022
"Blue Sky Somewhere," *Night to Dawn 41*, April, 2023
"Easy Prey", *Night to Dawn 45*, April, 2024
"Under a Dark Moon's Horn", *Night to Dawn 44*,
        2023
"Honors for My Lovers" *Star*Line*, Winter, 2022
"The Sinner", *Daily Science Fiction*, August 2nd, 2017

Previously Unpublished:

"People in the Sun"
"The Weather in Belize"
"The Color Purple"
"Frida's Bomb"
"Easy Prey"

Collaborations with Mary Turzillo:
"The Boyfriend", "The Child Remembers", "The Hat",
"SIRENS."

MARY TURZILLO:

"Crawl Space," *Bonsai Babies*, Omnium Gatherum,
        2016
"Vicious Trees," *Goblin Fruit*, October 9, 2007

"Solstice," *Lovers & Killers*, Dark Regions Press, 2012
"I Have Drunk" *Lovers & Killers*, Dark Regions Press,
    2012
"Pangs," as "Birth Pangs, Death Pangs," *HWA Show-
    case 2022*,
"FAQ," *Your Cat & Other Space Aliens*, Van Zeno,
    2007
"Black Roses, *Best of OPD 2013*, ed. Amy Jo Zook,
    Mechanicsburg, OH.
ALSO:
These two poems appeared previously in 2023 and are
Rhysling Award eligible for year 2023:
"We Must Be,"*Best of Ohio Poetry Day*, 2023.
"Ailurophobe," *The Weird Cat*, ed. Katherine Kerest -
    man and S. T. Joshi 2023, WordCrafts Press,
    2023.

Previously Published:

"Invisible"
"Little Brother, Big Sis"
"Fractal monster"
"Nighthawks"
"Two Wives"
"Prey Undo This Button"
"I Tread Rose Petals"
"Artists"
"Exorcism"
"A Gentlewoman to Save a Fallen Angel"
"Duel in the Dark"
"Diana and Guinevere"
"Heavy Metal"
"In the Dark House"
"Oblivio Mori"
"The Boyfriend" (Collaboration)
"The Hat" (Collaboration)
"The Child Remembers" (Collaboration)
"Sirens" (Collaboration)